M000013247

Presented To

_____

By

_____

Date

_____

The
POCKET DEVOTIONAL

Honor Books
Tulsa, Oklahoma

The Pocket Devotional
ISBN 1-56292-874-0

Copyright © 2002 by Honor Books, Inc.
P.O. Box 55388
Tulsa, Oklahoma 74155

Manuscript compiled by Patricia J. Lutherbeck, Tulsa, Oklahoma

Introduction

You owe it to yourself to take more time to reflect on God's principles, but how do you find the time? With *The Pocket Devotional,* you can feast on God's Word accompanied by a pertinent quotation and an upbeat reflection to help you apply these life-transforming principles to your life. Each day you will experience the uplifting inspiration that comes from reflecting on God's truth regularly.

The convenient size of this devotional makes it perfect to put in a purse or briefcase for those odd moments of the day, standing in line, waiting on a client, or over a cup of coffee on a break. It's small enough to put on the nightstand for that last quiet moment as you let go of the day's worries and let sleep overtake you. No matter where your available moments occur, *The Pocket Devotional* is small enough to carry along, just in case. Take it with you each day, and experience the life transformation that occurs when His truth sinks deep into your heart.

The most untutored person
with passion is more
persuasive than the
most eloquent without.

I know your eagerness to
help . . . your enthusiasm has
stirred most of them to action.

2 CORINTHIANS 9:2

Pursue Your Passion!

We've all been around people who bubble over with delight in their work, their hobby, or simply their life. We find their infectious enthusiasm hard to resist. The next thing we know, we get caught up in their excitement.

We've also known people who could make creation itself seem like just another string of scientific equations. For all their vast learning and impressive vocabulary, they've sacrificed the sense of wonder they were born with.

Which type of person would you rather listen to? Better yet, which type of person would you rather *be*? You don't need a highly educated mind or an eloquent tongue to live the abundant life and to pass it on. What you need is excitement about where God has placed you and what He has set before you.

Pursue your passions in life. Share your passion with others. Become known as a person of infectious enthusiasm.

When you stir a person's heart,
you touch their spirit as well.

Live so that you
wouldn't be ashamed
to sell the family parrot
to the town gossip.

*What you have said in the dark
will be heard in the daylight,
and what you have whispered in
the ear in the inner rooms will
be proclaimed from the roofs.*

LUKE 12:3

A Simple Test

There's a scary thought—having our private conversations shouted from the rooftops. Imagine every word we say in anger, every insult we hurl in triumph, every rumor we share in confidence amplified for all the world. That would find most of us trembling in fear.

Nothing gets us into hot water as quickly as our tongue. And nothing hurts others in quite the way our words do. Knowing this, you'd think we'd be better at controlling our speech, but old habits die hard.

Try this: For one day, notice every word you speak. (For some people, this alone could be a big challenge!) At the end of the day, you'll know how much of your daily speech is negative. The next day, ask God to help you increase your positive speech. Keep this up, and you just may lick those problems with your tongue.

The power of both good and evil is contained in the tongue—use it for good.

Two things fill the mind
with ever new and
increasing wonder and
awe—the starry heavens
above me and the
moral law within me.

*These liars have lied so well
and for so long that they've
lost their capacity for truth.*

1 TIMOTHY 4:2 THE MESSAGE

That Little Voice of Truth

What's the first thing most of us try to do when our conscience begins to bother us? We try to silence it! We figure that if we can't hear it anymore, it will just go away—but it won't.

Moreover, our conscience is another gift from God. It prompts us to do what's right and correct what's wrong. A clear conscience is essential if we expect to experience a joyful life.

A troubled conscience, however, creates a heavy weight that saps our energy, steals our joy, and damages our relationships. Why deny the offense we've committed? It won't work, and it will result in even greater anxiety in our spirit than the original offense. We need to give our conscience a chance to be heard so we can confess the wrong we've done, make restitution if necessary, and repair our broken relationships.

Make it a goal in your life to develop a highly sensitive conscience.

Patience is a quality you
admire in the driver
behind you and scorn
in the one ahead.

*The end of a matter is better
than its beginning, and patience
is better than pride. Do not be
quickly provoked in your spirit, for
anger resides in the lap of fools.*

Traffic in Pride

Traffic—it tests the patience of the even the most calm and collected of persons. If we suffer from chronic impatience, we don't stand a chance of winning the battle to behave when we're stuck behind an intolerably slow driver. Moreover, every time we try to be patient, some speeding maniac cuts us off! What can we do?

Hold on. The problem here isn't traffic. The problem is pride, which walks hand in hand with impatience. We feel that our need to get somewhere is more important than anyone else's. We defend that piece of pavement our car's tires are touching.

The next time you're stuck behind a slowpoke or cut off by a racer, pray for the other driver and for your own attitude. Ask God to reveal the way pride affects your driving—and your life. In time, you'll find more patience in other situations as well.

When you exercise patience in trying circumstances, people take notice.

The world does not understand theology or dogma, but it understands love and sympathy.

Now these three remain: faith, hope and love. But the greatest of these is love.

1 CORINTHIANS 13:13

Love and the Eyes of Faith

It may strike us as odd that the Bible rates love higher than faith. *How can that be?* we wonder. Doesn't God want to see evidence of mountain-moving, doubt-removing faith in His children? Yes, but first He wants to see a heart overflowing with love.

The God of the Bible has an infinite measure of compassion for each and every person who has ever lived—or ever will live. He loves without limit or condition. There isn't a single person who has ever experienced a day when God did not love him.

The problem is that most people don't realize God loves them. That's where we come in, and that's why the Bible says love is greater than both faith and hope. Our love—the love we have from God that flows out to others—is crucial in showing people the immeasurable love God has for them.

Love opens our eyes of faith
and gives us reason to hope.

It is good to remember that
the tea kettle, although up
to its neck in hot water,
continues to sing.

*Rejoice evermore. . . . In
every thing give thanks: for
this is the will of God in
Christ Jesus concerning you.*

1 THESSALONIANS 5:16-18 KJV

Trouble? Sing!

When we reach our boiling point, we should take that as a signal that it's time to sing. Well, maybe not literally *sing*, but at least call for a personal time out and remember all the things in our lives that give us cause for rejoicing.

If you're in a situation that has become so heated that you feel you're about to erupt, begin to thank God for the very circumstances that are causing you such grief. That doesn't mean you need to thank Him for the sin, abuse, misunderstanding, or illness that is plaguing you. Instead, thank God that the situation has driven you, needy, into His arms.

Clear your heart of angry, unforgiving thoughts. Allow God to heal that hurt. The peace He brings will make you want to sing again, and will keep you singing throughout your time of difficulty.

When we thank God during hard times, we open ourselves up to His inexpressible peace.

It's the little things in
life that determine
the big things.

*Thou hast been faithful over
a few things, I will make thee
ruler over many things: enter
thou into the joy of thy Lord.*

MATTHEW 25:21 KJV

Those Little Things

Sometimes it's hard to see the point in things we're required to do. Remember wondering in class why you had to learn something? Maybe as an adult you've never had to rattle off the principal export of Bolivia, but the time you spent in social studies class did teach you lots of other things; like patience, how to find the information you need, sticking to a routine, or simply obedience.

Those little things became big things in your daily life. The underlying principle—that little things add up to big things—works in your spiritual life also. Doing the little things like praying and reading your Bible creates a pattern of faithfulness that pleases God. You gain the courage to trust Him with those enormous, secret dreams you have. Be faithful in little things, and let Him astound you with the big things.

They may come a drop at a time, but your cup will eventually overflow with big blessings.

Ability will enable a man
to go to the top, but it
takes character to
keep him there.

The righteousness of the blameless
makes a straight way for them,
but the wicked are brought down
by their own wickedness.

PROVERBS 11:5

Making It to the Real Top

Yes, people have made it to the top through shady means, but are those people really at *the top?* Success is far more than reaching the highest rung on a ladder or commanding an impressive salary. Genuine success includes the ability to stand before God and the mirror with a clear conscience, and that comes from proven character.

Your integrity is pure gold in the eyes of God and other people. When you've proven yourself faithful and trustworthy, honest and forthright in *all* your dealings, you've reached a gratifying position in life—a place of honor and respect with your peers, your community, and your family. Cherish the reputation you've earned. Continue to depend on God to keep you blameless. He will draw others to Himself through you and the considerate trustworthiness they see. That's the top—and that's worth far more than a six-figure salary.

All the skills in the world can't make up for a deficit in character.

Jesus is a friend who knows all your faults and still loves you anyway.

God commendeth his love toward us, in that, while we were yet sinners, Christ died for us.

ROMANS 5:8 KJV

Love with No Strings Attached

If you've ever known someone who loved you unconditionally, you know what a treasure that is. Even in the most intimate relationships, however, no human being can possibly know all our faults. Only God has the ability to see the hidden secrets of our heart—those sins and faults that we skillfully manage to hide from others.

Astonishingly, God sees all that and loves us anyway. He loved us even before we became His children, when we were living a life that ignored Him completely. What's more, Jesus *died* for us, knowing everything about us—the good, the bad, and the ugly, and He loved us anyway.

We'll never have human love and acceptance that comes close to the love and acceptance Jesus offers. As we accept His friendship at ever-deepening levels of intimacy, He will show us how we can love others with fewer and fewer strings attached.

Offer the friendship of Jesus to your friends, no strings attached.

Never pass up a chance to
keep your mouth shut.

*Even a fool, when he holdeth
his peace, is counted wise: and
he that shutteth his lips is
esteemed a man of understanding.*

PROVERBS 17:28 KJV

Be Silent and Learn

Most people can say they've regretted the words that have come out of their mouths. Most of us can remember countless times when we said too much, said the wrong thing, or cracked a joke that left others in the room staring at us in an eternal silence. We love the sound of our own voices too much to let an opportunity for speech pass us by, regardless of the consequences.

When we let others do the talking—and we keep our ears open and mouths closed—it's amazing what we can learn: not just information, but insight into the deep, crying needs of others. Often, embedded in their words, is a need they can't express. In our silence, God has a chance to get His word in—to give us His wisdom—so that when we do open our mouths again, we'll truly have something worthwhile to give.

*Your silence can speak
volumes to a person in despair.*

Prayer should be the key
of the morning and the
lock of the night.

*It is good to praise the Lord
. . . to proclaim your love
in the morning and your
faithfulness at night.*

PSALM 92:1-2

The Way to Joy

Too often, we greet the day less-than-joyfully. For many of us, the overwhelming demands of twenty-first century life hit us when we first wake up; we have things to do, people to contact, and places to go. How can we possibly be joyful when our many responsibilities stare us in the face?

The answer lies in morning and evening prayer. The two go hand-in-hand. Morning prayer benefits us at night, while evening prayer blesses our morning. How? When we've prayed in the morning, we have a special opportunity to thank God at night for the way we saw Him working throughout the day. Our evening prayer time assures us that He is still in control while we sleep, so we can wake up refreshed, aware of His presence as we awake. That daily prayer cycle draws us closer to God with each day.

Unlock the door to your day and close the door at night by simply talking to God.

Self praise is no recommendation.

Let another man praise thee, and not thine own mouth; a stranger, and not thine own lips.

PROVERBS 27:2 KJV

Moving the Spotlight

Hearing people brag about their own accomplishment ranks in the top ten most annoying things other people do. It's also one of the top ten most annoying things *we* do. Let's face it, most of us are crying out to be admired and loved. We want to believe that our lives matter.

When we understand that truth, we can minister to others in a special and unique way. Are you in competition with a coworker for accolades or a promotion? Shine the spotlight on that person. Genuinely praise your coworker for a job well done. Apart from astonishing your coworkers, this will show the love of God in an extraordinary way. Is the person already so full of himself that he looks as if he's about to burst at the seams? That just reveals the depth of his need. Show him his life matters.

When you move the spotlight from yourself, God's light can shine into the lives of others.

Even if you're on the right track you'll get run over if you just sit there.

It isn't enough just to have faith. You must also do good to prove that you have it. Faith that doesn't show itself by good works is no faith at all—it is dead and useless.

JAMES 2:17 TLB

Believe—and Get Moving!

Dead and useless—pretty tough words to describe a person's faith. That's how the Bible describes the faith of *do-nothings,* people who express faith in God with words but do nothing tangible to minister to others. Meanwhile, hurting people cry out for help.

Look around you. If you live on planet earth, people in need surround you. Offer a cup of water to the thirsty, a meal to the hungry, encouragement to the hopeless. Give your time and money to ministries that can accomplish so much more with those combined resources.

Your words may put you on the right track, but there just could be a freight train headed your way. Get up and get moving! Your faith is worthless unless you are willing to put your legs and arms in motion for the benefit of others.

Your good works won't save you but they may lead others to the One who can save them.

Keep away from people who
try to belittle your ambitions.
Small people always do that,
but the really great people
make you feel that you,
too, can become great.

*Blessed is the man that walketh not
in the counsel of the ungodly, nor
standeth in the way of sinners, nor
sitteth in the seat of the scornful.*

PSALM 1:1 KJV

Don't Sacrifice That Dream!

At some point in our lives, we all had a really big dream or goal that we wanted to reach more than anything else we ever wanted. Maybe we shared that dream with someone, and all we got in return was an outburst of mocking laughter. Some people recover from humiliating incidents like that and go on to accomplish what they set out to do. Far too many, though, become crippled by the ridicule, giving up altogether.

People who ridicule others' ambitions are plagued by insecurity. Their mockery has more to do with their own sense of failure. Once we understand that, it's easy to pick ourselves up and keep working toward our goal. Along the way, we *will* meet encouragers, those people who are so secure that they're able to cheer us on to our own finish line.

Never sacrifice your dream to those who envy your efforts at success.

Carefully guard your dreams from those who would rob you of them.

Weakness of attitude becomes weakness of character.

Do not be conformed to this world, but be transformed by the renewing of your mind, that you may prove what is that good and acceptable and perfect will of God.

ROMANS 12:2 NKJV

Navigating by a Fixed Point

Any pilot knows the attitude of a plane is determined by its position in relation to a fixed point on the horizon or in the heavens. Come to think of it, our attitude is determined in a similar way.

When we fix our eyes on God—the only One who is the same yesterday, today, and forever—we find it easier to maintain a steady, positive attitude. When we take our eyes off Him, we wobble and veer off course. Our loss of direction shows up in our attitude; and before we know it, our character is affected.

As you navigate your way through your day, keep your attitude in check. Staying the course gives a much smoother ride. Others will adjust their attitude to yours, especially if you are in a position of authority. Your renewed mind can transform the atmosphere in your home, your workplace, and your church.

Keep your eyes fixed on
the One who never changes.

You see things; and you say, "Why?" But I dream things that never were; and I say, "Why not?"

Without faith it is impossible to please God.

HEBREWS 11:6

Living in the Extreme

Imagine putting all your heart into doing something to impress God—only to discover that your mere human efforts failed to please Him because you failed to trust Him to do even greater things *through* you with His spiritual energy. That would be pretty disheartening; but many people live their lives this way, without ever realizing that their lack of faith makes it impossible for them to please God no matter how hard they try.

When God pinpoints the task He has for you, allow your faith in Him to expand to equal the task. A life of faith is a life lived in the extreme—an adventure that will sometimes leave you breathless and awed by the wonder-working power of the Creator of the universe. That's the way God designed us to live. To settle for anything less is to miss out on a genuine once-in-a-lifetime opportunity.

*Let God do through you what
you could never do yourself!*

You can't hold a man
down without staying
down with him.

The man who sets a trap for
others will get caught in it himself.

PROVERBS 26:27 TLB

Don't Set Traps!

Trappers know that just about the most important thing about setting traps is remembering where they are. You don't ever want to forget that. If you do, one day you may find your leg caught in the very device you had set to catch a critter.

Be careful if you're thinking about setting a plan in motion to *trap* someone. Troublesome people are not like animals, and the traps we set for other people have a way of tripping us. Is someone in your family being a real pest? See him for the broken, needy person he is. Would you just love to catch a coworker who's getting by with murder? Look inside your own heart first, and leave the sleuthing to those in charge. You have nothing to gain and everything to lose by seeking the downfall of others.

Give yourself the gift of a clear conscience by refusing to set a trap.

From the errors of others
the wise man corrects his
own.

*Where there is no counsel,
the people fall; But in the
multitude of counselors
there is safety.*

PROVERBS 11:14 NKJV

Avoid That Nightmare!

Have you ever known someone who walked right into a nightmare—a bad marriage, for instance—after refusing to listen to the wisdom of others? Most of us have been in a situation like that. We've either been the one who refused to seek advice, or the one whose counsel was ignored. Either way, it hurts—especially when the consequences are severe.

We sabotage our chances for a successful, joyful life when we choose to rely only on our own instincts, intelligence, and wisdom. No one person could possibly know everything. Yes, there will be times when others seem to thwart our attempts to accomplish what is clearly God's will; and yes, there will be times when our trusted counselors will offer conflicting advice. We must never let the exceptions stand in the way of the overriding principle: There *is* wisdom in many counselors.

*Surround yourself with people
whose counsel you trust.*

He slept beneath the moon,
He basked beneath the sun;
He lived a life of going-to-do,
And died with nothing done.

He who gathers crops in summer is a wise son, but he who sleeps during harvest is a disgraceful son.

A Time to Get Moving

Timing, they say, is everything. The Bible confirms this: There *is* a time for every purpose under heaven. To paraphrase Ecclesiastes, there's a time to dream and a time to stop dreaming and get to work. Dreaming—allowing the creative part of your mind to wander in a productive way—can be fruitful. Excessive dreaming, however, amounts to idleness.

Has your mind stumbled onto the perfect solution to a nagging problem? Put that solution to work. Do you have an innovative idea for ministering to the homeless? It's time to put your theory to the test.

Following through with an inspirational thought means hard work, and seeing a project through to its completion requires perseverance to plow through obstacles. Few worthwhile things in life come without a fair amount of perspiration and persistence. If this is your time, act on it now. The harvest you'll reap will far outweigh the effort you expend.

Every dreamer needs to wake up eventually.

A poor man is not that
one without a cent.
A poor man is that one
without a dream.

*The intelligent man is
always open to new ideas.
In fact, he looks for them.*

PROVERBS 18:15 TLB

Step Out and Move Up

In recent decades, the business world was jolted into a new economic reality: Companies that relied only on the tried and true failed. Innovation became the lifeblood for any organization that wished to keep its head above water. With astonishing speed, businesses most open to innovation—which sometimes looked like complete lunacy—moved to the top of the heap.

We need innovation in our personal lives too. Yes, biblical principles do not change, but the methods we use to apply those principles change as our culture changes. If you've tried to parent a teenager today the way your parents or grandparents did in the past, you know how ineffective the supposedly tried-and-true can be.

Embrace change. Seek new ideas. Adapt to new methods. Maintaining the status quo will only keep you in a rut, and that's not where real life is lived. Step out of your rut—and move up.

Let the light of new ideas
shine through your life.

There is no security in life,
only opportunity.

*We know that in all things
God works for the good
of those who love him.*

ROMANS 8:28

Create Opportunity

As many people learned in recent years, job security is a thing of the past. Even where you can still find company loyalty, you can't count on company longevity. Many who expected to retire after a lifetime with the same company found themselves downsized into a whole new career choice, but others found themselves in unemployment lines.

What made the difference in those two groups? Opportunity. Some, to be sure, had it handed to them, but many who found new careers created their own opportunity. Many who went on unemployment seemed to have no other choice, but within their ranks were lots of people who failed to recognize opportunity.

If we really believe that all things work together for good, then we must apply that to misfortune as well. Events that at first seem bleak can steer us in an exciting new direction if we keep our eyes, ears, and mind open.

What exciting opportunity are you facing right now?

God's in His Heaven
All's right with the world.

*If God is for us,
who can be against us?*

ROMANS 8:31

True Optimism

Are you a pessimist or an optimist? That's not an easy question for most people. You may consider yourself an optimist—until you take another look at the world around you. Then, you'd have to admit, it's hard to be hopeful.

Hold on. Looking at what's going on in the world is never going to offer you hope, and that's not where you should direct your attention. Difficulties only loom larger when you're in a negative frame of mind.

True optimists can face difficulties because they've learned a vital lesson: Nothing can come our way that's too big for God to handle. He's never surprised by our challenges, and He's not going to leave us alone, either. We have no need to fear our future, our troubles, or our enemies. God *is* for us, and He'll handle the things that come against us—no matter how insurmountable they appear.

*An optimist has learned
to look up, not around.*

It is a mistake to look too far ahead. Only one link of the chain of destiny can be handled at one time.

Why, you do not even know what will happen tomorrow. What is your life? You are a mist that appears for a little while and then vanishes.

JAMES 4:14

Live for Tomorrow . . . Today!

You've heard people say this—maybe even yourself: "If God would only show me what's going to happen in the future, I'd know what decisions to make now." God knows everything, so why won't He tell us?

We know at least one answer to that question: We wouldn't need faith, and our faith pleases God. There's another answer, however. If we knew everything coming our way, we couldn't handle it.

Without God's help, we can't know the future—so why try to look ahead? Don't we have enough to concern us right here and now? Why do we attempt to add to our already overburdened lives? We'd all be better off if we'd focus on the present—the urgent tasks, important responsibilities, and wonderful possibilities that each day holds. We have exactly what we need to make it through life one day at a time.

You can plan for the future without trying to see into it first.

Man's extremity is
God's opportunity.

*With God nothing
is ever impossible.*

LUKE 1:37 AMP

Yes, I Can!

"*You* can't do that!" We've heard it, and we may have even said it ourselves. Our intentions were good. Maybe we were afraid that our friends or loved ones would lose their shirts by starting a new business, or we thought it would be too dangerous for our children to move to a distant city to start a new career. We may have only interfered with the purpose they were intended to fulfill.

When you're on the receiving end of discouraging comments, it's hard to keep your focus on your goal or path. If you're convinced you're doing what God has placed before you—and if people you trust are cheering you on—then achieving your goal is far from impossible, no matter what the naysayers believe. Keep looking straight ahead. Think of the pleasure you'll experience when you can finally turn around and say, "Oh yes *I* can!"

Remove the word "impossible" from your daily thoughts and conversation.

The evening of a
well-spent life brings
its lamps with it.

*As the days of a tree, so
will be the days of my people;
my chosen ones will long enjoy
the works of their hands.*

ISAIAH 65:22

Keep It Simple

There's no question about it: If you're still breathing, then God is not finished with you yet. Not only is He still refining your character, He's also setting before you countless opportunities to fulfill the purpose for which He placed you on Earth.

Don't know your purpose? Start with a few responsibilities that every believer has: praying for others, sharing the God's love and meeting needs in whatever way you can, getting to know God more intimately, discovering how He speaks to you, and learning to obey when He nudges you to do something. In no time, you'll know His purpose for you.

It's easy to fall into the trap of complicating our lives. We think if we don't follow this leader's four-step process or that speaker's six-step plan, we'll miss God's will. God never intended our lives to be so complex. If we simply obey Him, His plan will unfold.

Mission impossible? Not if it's from God.

Short as life is, we
make it shorter by the
careless waste of time.

*Man is like a breath; his
days are like a fleeting shadow.*

PSALM 144:4

Redeem the Time

Remember when each day seemed to last forever—especially each school day? Our distorted sense of time as children is a temporary gift. It's hard to comprehend how short life is when we're ten, and the thing we want most in life is a driver's license. Each year seems like an eternity.

As we age, it begins to dawn on us that life really doesn't last forever. For many, the realization doesn't hit with full force until middle age. By then we've lost decades time.

No matter how old—or young—you still have a chance to redeem that time. Take account of how you spend your days. What unnecessary activities drain away minutes and hours that could be better spent? Even the time spent in genuine relaxation is more beneficial than mere idleness. Make use of the time left to you, and you'll have fewer regrets as the years pass by.

Don't shorten your years by wasting your days.

To know is not to be wise . . .
There is no fool so great as a
knowing fool. But to know
how to use knowledge
is to have wisdom.

*The fear of the Lord is the
beginning of knowledge, but fools
despise wisdom and discipline.*

PROVERBS 1:7

The Partner of Knowledge

It's so easy to get this one backwards. With our contemporary emphasis on education, we relentlessly pursue knowledge, seldom placing any importance on gaining the partner of knowledge: wisdom. Our technology features all the latest bells and whistles, but our use of technology spins out of ethical control.

Why? Because so little of our knowledge holds an understanding of God's purpose for humanity. Without that wisdom, our great learning amounts to little more than foolishness, a dangerous foolishness that begins a slide into moral decay.

Should we stop seeking knowledge? No, but we should approach what we learn through the grid of the God's wisdom. That means remembering what we know about God and what He reveals in the Bible as we open ourselves to new ideas and information. Remember—God is always on hand to clear up anything we don't understand.

Wisdom teaches us how to
interpret everything we've learned.

We cannot be guilty
of a greater act of
uncharitableness than to
interpret the afflictions which
befall our neighbors as
punishment and judgment.

*Stop judging by mere appearances,
and make a right judgment.*

JOHN 7:24

Safe Judgment

Life happens. The sun shines and the rain falls on the good and evil alike. Our good fortune is no more an indication of our righteousness than our neighbor's bad fortune is of his unrighteousness. If the opposite were true, then drug-addicted athletes and celebrities would be broke—not the multimillionaires that they are—and those who faithfully serve God would never experience pain, sorrow, financial loss, or fatal disease.

Judging people on any level is outside the scope of our responsibilities as believers. God is the only one who has the final authority to judge, and He doesn't need our help to accomplish that. What He does ask is that we serve as His heart on earth, loving people and revealing His love to them.

The only safe judgment you can make about a person is that he needs God. The best way to help meet that need is to look beyond appearances and offer him the same love you've received from the Father.

*Be thankful when people resist
the temptation to judge you.*

The trouble with modern
civilization is that
we so often mistake
respectability for character.

*Man looks at the outward
appearance, but the
LORD looks at the heart.*

1 SAMUEL 16:7

Beyond Image

It wasn't long ago when peoples' jobs, standing in the community, or positions in church meant that they were respectable. Onlookers naturally assumed that if you maintained a certain public image, you were, without a doubt, a person of character.

As painful as it's been to see prominent people in all walks of life toppled from their positions by moral failure, we can all learn a valuable lesson in the process: Outward appearances do not guarantee character. While that makes it more difficult to determine which people you can trust, it makes it easier to recognize the importance of trusting in God.

You can't see a person's heart, but if you know the One who can, you can rely on Him when you need to know about someone's trustworthiness. People can be fooled by appearances, but God is never deceived by the condition of a person's heart.

Remembering where to place your trust can keep you from being deceived.

Kindness has converted
more people than zeal,
science, or eloquence.

*Or do you show contempt for
the riches of his kindness,
tolerance and patience, not
realizing that God's kindness
leads you toward repentance?*

ROMANS 2:4

The Kindness of God

Even if you came to faith in God through an overwhelming sense of your own sinfulness or fear of eternal separation from Him, at some point God's kindness came into play. The act of extending unconditional love and forgiveness demonstrates His kind nature.

We can take a cue from God when we bring others to Him. A simple act of kindness can go a long way toward showing people God's love, especially in a society where so many are wary of offering or receiving help.

Cashiers, waitresses, waiters, and customer service representatives often see more hostility and hear more anger in a single day than others do in a full week. Go out of your way to be courteous and pleasant. Don't forget to be kind, patient, and tolerant with your family as well—they may be the ones who need it most.

All the zeal in the world won't compensate for a single unkind act.

Conformity is the
jailer of freedom and
the enemy of growth.

*Do not conform any longer
to the pattern of this world,
but be transformed by the
renewing of your mind.*

ROMANS 12:2

Be Different and Make a Difference!

A wonderful transformation takes place when we accept Christ into our lives. We begin to see things from a different perspective; but somehow, being different in today's society is often viewed as a negative quality.

Don't let anyone imprison you in a cell of conformity. You may be the one who holds the key to transforming your neighborhood, workplace, or community for Christ. Be willing to step out of your comfort zone. God created and then re-created you to be a unique individual, with talents, gifts, and experiences that He can use for His purposes.

Give God access to your creativity and imagination to grow your faith. You may be surprised at the freedom you experience—and at the innovative ways in which He directs your life. Never be afraid to be different; after all, Jesus was the most different person who ever lived, and our goal should be to become like Him.

Celebrate your uniqueness by refusing to conform.

There are enough targets
to aim at without
firing at each other.

*Be kind and compassionate to one
another, forgiving each other, just
as in Christ God forgave you.*

EPHESIANS 4:32

Fight the Fight

Battles are waged more often among believers themselves, rather than against the forces of evil in the world. What's up with that? Doesn't the Bible say we should love one another, and that the world will know we are followers of Jesus by the love we show to each other? Yes, it does, and often we fall short.

What can we do to reverse this? We can stop taking potshots at each other. We can fight the fight, by making a conscious decision to avoid all infighting, and also by offering ourselves as peacemakers when disputes surface. We can resolve to be among those who do not gossip, slander, or stir up strife. We can immediately forgive offenses, both little and big.

Every little step we take individually toward reconciliation and loving relationships with other believers becomes a giant leap when others join us. That's love the world can see.

Be a light to the world—fight the fight.

We are never defeated,
unless we give up on God.

*No, in all these things we
are more than conquerors
through him who loved us.*

The Dark Night of the Soul

How often have you sung about victory or heard people talk about the victorious Christian life and felt utterly defeated inside? If you're like most Christians, that's happened more often than you'd like to admit. Even some of the greatest saints in church history have gone through times when they felt far from triumphant.

The key to regaining the victory is to never give up on God, regardless of how we feel at the moment. We can go through our dark night of the soul, when nothing seems to be working and evil forces seem to draw closer and closer. We can emerge even stronger in our faith, as long as we never cease seeking God. He is always near to us, even when He seems far away—and He will give us the power to become more than conquerors, no matter how hopeless the battle seems.

When you feel overwhelmed,
turn to the One who overcomes.

Marriage has in it less of beauty, but more of safety, than the single life. It has more care, but less danger; it is more merry, and more sad. It is fuller of sorrows, and fuller of joys; it lies under more burdens, but it is supported by all the strengths of love, and charity, and those burdens are delightful.

For this reason a man will leave his father and mother and be united to his wife, and the two will become one flesh.

EPHESIANS 5:31

Think Together

We're never satisfied with what we have. We fall in love with a person who has so many qualities that we admire—qualities we wish we could lay claim to. Then, within a few years, we wish that same person, now our spouse, would think more like we do. In time, the word "incompatible" starts to creep into our thoughts about our marriage.

Most differences between a husband and wife, though, represent strength, not weakness. Once we come to terms with this, we can stop trying to think alike and start putting our heads together to come up with creative solutions to problems in our relationship and in our life together.

Don't expect your spouse to be like you. Instead, cherish the individual distinctions that, when combined, create a whole new creation in marriage. When you allow this new creation to flourish, you strengthen your marriage and find unity.

Two heads joined in loving relationship
are definitely better than one.

In taking revenge a man is
but even with his enemy;
but in passing it over,
he is superior.

Do not repay anyone evil for evil.
Be careful to do what is
right in the eyes of everybody.

ROMANS 12:17

The Price of Payback

Any act of revenge, no matter how justified, is just plain ugly. Behind it is a bitter person who has chosen to sink to the lowest level on the rungs of justice. Rage wins out over reason; vengeance over forgiveness. It's payback time, and there's no chance for a merciful sentence.

What many vengeful people seldom take into account is the toll revenge takes on them. They're so focused on hurting someone else that they can't see the damage they're doing to themselves. Medical studies have shown time and again that vindictive people suffer from numerous physical problems brought on by clinging to anger. On the other hand, people who forgive experience those ailments less often and less severely.

Why not pass over the offense and live a healthier, more peaceful life? In doing so, you will also please God and reveal to others the moral, forgiving quality of His character in you.

Be healthy—forgive!

What is the use of praying if at
the very moment of prayer we
have so little confidence in God
that we are busy planning our own
kind of answer to our prayer?

Do not be anxious about anything,
but in everything, by prayer
and petition, with thanksgiving,
present your requests to God.

PHILIPPIANS 4:6

Helping God?

Many of us try to help God along by coming up with our own ideas about the very best way He could answer our prayers, and then expect Him to follow our plan. Even worse, we pray and then dismiss Him entirely as we take the matter into our own hands. What's the point?

When we present our requests to God, a second step is required—leaving them in His care. Simply stating the problem or asking for help is not enough. We have to put it into his hands and walk away. That seems almost rude, but it's what He wants. He knows that we cannot serve and love Him; or serve and love other people if we are distracted. By freeing ourselves from concern we are free to obey. He really does want us to cast all our cares on Him.

The best sign of trust in God is the ability to leave our cares in His hands.

The power of a man's virtue
should not be measured
by his special efforts,
but by his ordinary doing.

*Live such good lives among pagans
that, though they accuse you of
doing wrong, they may see your
good deeds and glorify God.*

1 PETER 2:12

Extraordinary in the Ordinary

People can argue with your faith, your doctrine, and even your convictions, but one thing they can never successfully dispute is a life well lived.

Your day-to-day activities speak volumes about the supernatural nature of the Christian life. An ordinary person who honorably, faithfully, and selflessly serves God in full view of a watching world is more likely to lead someone to a lasting faith in Christ than the most eloquent preacher on the planet. An ordinary person's faith can demonstrate the powerful truth behind mere words.

Make sure your life reveals the miracle-working power of the living God. It's not enough for us to simply be good, moral, respectable, or virtuous; we need to be a walking, talking, breathing Exhibit A—evidence of the life-transforming power that is available to everyone. Let your example give them cause to glorify God.

Your life is on display for others to see—make sure it points them to God.

The heart once fairly given to God with a clear conscience, a fitting rule of life, and a steadfast purpose of obedience, you will find a wonderful sense of rest coming over you.

He makes me lie down in green pastures, he leads me beside quiet waters, he restores my soul.

PSALM 23:2-3

Take a Break! Signed, God

How often do you give yourself the pleasure of just resting in the presence of God? There's nothing wrong with that. As pastor and author Henry Blackaby expresses it, sometimes God says to us, "Don't just do something—stand there!" Instead, we go on in our busyness, fearing that if we aren't doing something for God, we aren't pleasing Him.

But our obedience pleases God, and sometimes what He wants us to do is take a break and rest awhile— especially when we've experienced failure or defeat. The time will come soon enough when we need to get back on our feet and get back to work. He'll let us know when the time is right for that. When our soul needs restoration, however, He'll lead us to those green pastures and quiet waters that provide the peace and tranquility we so desperately long for.

Don't resist the rest and relaxation God offers. It's a precious gift, held in reserve for us when we need it most.

Obey your Father when
He tells you it's nap time!

The well of Providence is deep. It's the buckets we bring to it that are small.

Look at the birds of the air
. . . your heavenly Father
feeds them. Are you not
much more valuable than they?

MATTHEW 6:26

Get a Big Bucket!

How big is your bucket? That's an odd question to ask someone, but it's a question we should all ask ourselves. When we go to the well to get what we need, do we bring a big, watertight bucket, knowing that the well is bottomless; or do we bring a teaspoon, half believing that we're not worthy of any more than that? *I shouldn't expect much,* we think. *After all, I'll just spill it on the way home anyway.*

The Father's resources are limitless and available to everyone in His family. You can't possibly take too much, but you can certainly take too little. A misunderstanding of the nature of humility may cause you to think you're not entitled to all that God has for you. Remember that He gives out of His love for us, not because of anything we've done to earn His generosity. He *wants* to give, and He wants you to come and get what He has just for you.

All of God's gifts are yours for the taking.

Whatever you dislike in another person, take care to correct in yourself.

Why do you look at the speck of sawdust in your brother's eye and pay no attention to the plank in your own eye?

MATTHEW 7:3

Look at You!

There's truth in the belief that what irritates us the most in other people is exactly what we do ourselves. However, we sometimes don't recognize our own guilt. Maybe it galls you when your coworker interrupts you when you're talking; but then you get home and finish every sentence for your spouse. That seems different, but it isn't. The irritations are identical.

The next time someone really starts to get on your nerves, take a good, hard, honest look at the situation. Can't you see at least a little bit of yourself in the person who's been bugging you? If so, that's great! You can finally start working on that flaw in your own character. Work to catch yourself every time you behave in the way that bothers you so much in other people. Then, work on changing the habit that is giving you one enormous headache.

You'll feel much better once you get that plank out of your eye!

Any man may commit a mistake, but none but a fool will continue in it.

Though a righteous man falls seven times, he rises again, but the wicked are brought down by calamity.

PROVERBS 24:16

Get On With Life

It's hard to admit we're wrong, especially if we've argued heatedly and adamantly maintained our point of view. Then when we realize we've made a mistake—that the very thing we argued for was actually wrong—it's embarrassing to have to take it all back. It's easier to continue pretending that we know we're right.

That's pride. Granted, maybe we shouldn't have been so hotheaded, but what's done is done. It's time to admit our mistake, make our apologies, and get on with our life.

That principle holds true for other mistakes as well. If you've gotten involved in a business or taken a job that was clearly a mistake, don't prolong the error by failing to admit your error. Make whatever changes you must make, without hurting others in the process. Then learn from your mistake and get on with the life you were meant to live.

Don't be brought down by your mistakes—learn from them instead.

Every individual has a
place to fill in the world,
and is important, in
some respect, whether he
chooses to be so or not.

*I know the thoughts and plans that
I have for you, says the Lord,
thoughts and plans for welfare
and peace, and not for evil, to give
you hope in your final outcome.*

JEREMIAH 29:11 AMP

Your Unique Mission

Do you believe you have a special purpose in life, one that only you can fulfill? Whether or not your place in this world looks important to you, it is.

By making each person unique, God intended for each of us to play specific role in life. While lots of people go through life ignorant of their ultimate purpose, it doesn't have to be that way. Look where God has placed you right now—within a certain family, living in a particular neighborhood, interacting with a specific set of people on a daily basis; and if you are a parent, nurturing and shaping another human being.

Failing to recognize your place in the world can tempt you to feel your daily life is insignificant. Remember, you have a sphere of influence that no one else has—and that alone makes your life vitally important.

You are the only one who can fulfill your unique mission in life.

No worldly success
can compensate for
failure in the home.

*Children, obey your parents in
the Lord, for this is right . . .
And you, fathers, do not provoke
your children to wrath, but bring
them up in the training and
admonition of the Lord.*

EPHESIANS 6:1-4 NKJV

Children and Time

We hear it all the time–parents must spend time with their children. Younger children obviously need more attention, but to think our preteens and teenagers can fend for themselves is a mistake. Sure, they may act as if they don't need us, but they do–whether they realize it or not.

Making a living, serving in church, maintaining a household–all these things drain the time we should be giving our children. Often we feel little control over those things that crowd our schedule, but if we've lost control to that extent, the problem lies with us, not with the schedule. We need to look carefully at how we spend our time. What activities can be eliminated? How can we include our children in some of the time-consuming tasks for which we're responsible? It's never too late to make changes that may secure a child's future.

You'll never regret placing your children above your other commitments in life.

With the fearful strain that is on me night and day, if I did not laugh I should die.

Our light affliction, which is but for a moment, worketh for us a far more exceeding and eternal weight of glory.

2 CORINTHIANS 4:17 KJV

Laugh!

Lighten up! There are few situations in life that can't be improved by a good, healthy sense of humor. We take things so seriously these days. People are all too easily offended. We're ready to sue at the drop of a hat—or shake our fists in self-righteous anger at some injustice. We're thin-skinned, thickheaded, and not a lot of fun to be with.

Yes, there are some very serious problems in our world. All the more reason to keep it light when it comes to the less important things. Can you remember a catastrophe in your past that you approached as if the world was coming to an end? The world just kept on spinning, though, and now you can probably chuckle at your reaction now. Look at your present circumstances in the same way—and realize that down the road, you'll look back in amusement.

Maintaining a sense of humor will help you weather the storms of life.

Fear can keep a person
out of danger, but courage
can support them in it.

*We have this hope as an anchor
for the soul, firm and secure.*

HEBREWS 6:19

Find an Anchor

People securely anchored are those who exhibit the greatest measure of grace in the pressure cooker. Some of America's greatest military leaders made their country proud not only by the soundness of their strategy, but also by the strength of their character. In the face of unrelenting life-and-death pressure, they maintained their resolve. They were anchored in their purpose.

We can have that same cool resolve if we anchor our hope in God. The pressure to succeed, to do twice as much in a single day than is possible, even the pressure to cut corners to get a job done—all of these stresses weigh on us and tempt us. We can have the hope and security that keep us steadfast when those winds and waves pound against us. We will be the ones most likely to remain calm in situations that make others crumble.

You don't need to muster up courage
when your soul is anchored in God.

Anxiety does not empty
tomorrow of its sorrows,
but only empties
today of its strength.

*Cast your cares on the Lord
and he will sustain you.*

PSALM 55:22

Send It to God

Anxiety takes us a good step or two beyond worry to a gnawing sense of dread and apprehension. What's worse, sometimes we have no clue what causes such fear. We feel that something terrible will happen, and we can do nothing about it. Maybe we can't do anything about the things we dread, but we can do something about the anxiety.

Start dealing with it by finding the cause of the anxiety. It may be something you actually do have control over; or it may be something that makes you wonder why you felt apprehensive. You may never determine what it is. Regardless, you know in your heart what you have to do—that's right, give it to God. If you've tried but failed, visualize the problem in your hand, put it in a box and tie it shut. Float it up to Him, releasing it as you pray.

When anxious thoughts come your way, send them on to God.

A transformed life is the everyday miracle that testifies to the presence of God in the universe.

Hold on to instruction, do not let it go; guard it well, for it is your life.

PROVERBS 4:13

The Gift of Change

How are things in your corner of the universe? Is everything going well, or are you at odds with people who are beyond your control? Most likely, even people under your control—like your children—could use a little improvement. You can teach them, train them, and threaten them; but when all is said and done, you cannot force them to change against their will. The human will is too strong and, sometimes, too stubborn.

That leaves only one person you can change—yourself. But how strong is your will? How stubborn are you? A strong will is a good thing to have when you need to stand up for your convictions. If you need to change, however, then stubbornness and a strong will can stand in your way. The solution? Bend your will toward God, and let Him change you. He is the only one with control.

Change is God's gift to you—
seek Him and you will find it.

Identify your highest
skill and devote your
time to performing it.

*Give diligence to make your calling
and election sure: for if ye do
these things, ye shall never fall.*

2 PETER 1:10 KJV

The Rule of Mastery

Diligence—working with steady and even exacting effort—often separates one who has mastered a skill from one who has merely learned it. Yes, there are those rare Mozarts who sit down at a piano at the age of four and flawlessly create a complex masterpiece. The rule holds, however, that most people who gain mastery—whether it's in sculpting, teaching, accounting, or carpentry—achieve it by applying themselves, sometimes obsessively, to their passion in life.

Mastery of skills gives tremendous satisfaction. You own that skill, and no one can take it away from you. In the same way, you can apply diligence to your Christian walk. When you give careful attention and concentrated effort to Bible reading, prayer, and service, you gain something that no one can take: God's wisdom hidden in your heart, and an intimate friendship with the Master of all things.

There is no higher mastery than getting to know the Master.

Every man dies;
not every man lives.

*I came that they may have life,
and have it abundantly.*

JOHN 10:10 NASB

Want More?

If someone were to ask why Jesus came to earth, you'd answer: "He came to save us all from eternal punishment." You'd be right, but there's more: He also came to give us life in the here-and-now, an abundant life.

Many of us feel more like we're hanging by a thread. Abundant life? What's that? All we see is work, bills, family problems, and worse, boredom. Maybe Sunday mornings feel better, and occasionally we've seen God work in our lives; but the abundant life seems to have passed us by on a daily basis.

Your heart yearns for more, but you don't know what to do about it? Give yourself completely to God. Then follow your heart. You have permission to do that. The Bible says that God will give you the desires of your heart when your heart is turned toward Him.

God gave you the dream for an abundant life that resides in your heart.

Self-control is the ability to keep cool while someone is making it hot for you.

A soft answer turns away wrath, but grievous words stir up anger.

PROVERBS 15:1 AMP

Whisper!

The best way to get someone's attention is to whisper. Somehow, we have difficulty remembering that in a heated argument with someone, or in a group of unruly kids. Shouting seems to be the only way to ensure being heard. This method usually backfires, though, only serving to prolong the now overheated argument and to give the kids even more reason to be disruptive.

Next time you're tempted to raise your voice: Don't. Instead, keep your cool. While you're counting to ten, think of the gentlest response you can possibly give. Then quietly deliver it with all the grace and dignity you can muster—not haughtiness or arrogance. Most people will be so amazed at your demeanor that they will back off immediately. Your soft answer will pave the way for a genuine resolution, and you will score a victory in the battle to maintain your self-control.

Keep practicing until you have nothing but soft answers to give.

Avoiding danger is no safer in the long run than outright exposure. Life is either daring adventure or nothing.

I have told you these things, so that in me you may have peace. In this world you will have trouble. But take heart! I have overcome the world.

JOHN 16:33

Walk on Water!

Is your life a daring adventure, or do you try to play it safe—avoiding all risk? You can't avoid all risk, and sometimes God tells you to get out of the boat and dare to walk on water. Will you take a chance, or will you try to stay safe and warm in the boat?

Peter knew the only place he could be genuinely safe was in the Lord's presence—and sometimes, that meant risk. Others may hang back and rely on the resources of the world for shelter from the storms, but those who have a heart of trust know that nothing can come against them that God can't control—even storms.

You only have one life; why not turn it into an exciting adventure? Place your faith completely in God. Climb out of that cozy boat, and start walking on water! You'll never regret it.

Playing it safe is just another way of living a faithless life.

My temptations have
been my masters
in divinity.

*Perseverance must finish its work
so that you may be mature and
complete, not lacking in anything.*

JAMES 1:4

Keeping On

God seldom calls us into a significant ministry without, at some point, testing our ability to withstand pressure. Not only does this confirm His faithfulness, but also it demonstrates what we're made of inside. If we can't handle the pressure of everyday difficulties, those of ministry will no doubt swamp us, taking the ministry down with us as well.

If God ordained the faith journey on which you've embarked, persevere through the obstacles that come your way, and rejoice! That's right—rejoice that God is strengthening you, steeling you for the long road ahead. The pressures involved in serving God can be immense—financial concerns, expectations of others, heartbreaking needs of those you're called to serve, unrelenting demands on your time and your family, and the inevitable spiritual attacks and temptations. You need to be strong, and you need to be prepared. God wants to show you that in Him you're equal to the task.

Keep on keeping on with the mission God has placed before you.

Hope has a thick skin and will endure many a blow; it will put on patience as a vestment; it will wade through a sea of blood; it will endure all things if it be of the right kind, for the joy that is set before it.

So now, go. I am sending you to Pharaoh to bring my people the Israelites out of Egypt.

EXODUS 3:10

Fat Chance?

Of all the people in history who have had little tangible reason to hope, Moses has to be in the top ten. The likelihood that Pharaoh would let the Israelites leave Egypt was not even measurable. "Fat chance!" is probably what Moses heard when he shared God's plans. Pharaoh was relentless. Despite the mighty acts of God, he would not let this nation of cheap laborers out of his sight, following them all the way to a supposedly uncrossable sea.

Moses, of course, had no faith in Pharaoh. He had faith and hope that God would make good on His promise and set Israel free. Had he backed down along about the fifth plague, the Israelites would have missed out on an incomparable miracle of God's provision.

Have you lost hope? Don't give up—ever. Next year, next month, and even the next hour may bring the answer you long for.

*There are no hopeless situations
when God is involved.*

When you come to
the end of your rope,
tie a knot and hang on.

*Cast all your anxiety on him
because he cares for you.*

1 PETER 5:7

Climb Out of Depression

When we allow anxiety to rule our lives, we become more and more prone to chronic depression, an ongoing mental condition that negatively colors everything in the world around us. We cease to function normally. We become paralyzed in our walk with God and in our relationships with other people. Everything looks bleak.

If you are in this condition, or you know anyone else who is, the time for help is now. Confess your depression to God and to a pastor or trusted counselor; don't wait until you begin to feel better. Immerse yourself in the Bible, concentrating on those verses that describe who you are in God. Lay down every anxious, self-deprecating, and negative thought. Replace those thoughts with what God says about you.

You are precious—vitally important—so significant that God sent His Son to die for you. Never forget that crucial truth about yourself.

Surround yourself with others who know who you are in God's sight.

A ship in harbor is safe,
but that is not what
ships are built for.

*You are the world's light——a city
on a hill, glowing in the night for
all to see. Don't hide your light!*

MATTHEW 5:14-15 TLB

Go! And Don't Worry

As believers we are called to get out of our safety zone and share our faith in God with others. Many of us shudder at the thought. The questions seem unending: What will we say? How will people respond to us? What if they laugh at us or even hurt us physically? What if no one turns toward God?

It's important to keep in mind that we are called to *go*, and not worry about what will happen when we do. God will take care of the results if we will act in obedience, ask for His will to be accomplished, and give our plans to Him so that He may direct our path.

Your life is a testimony to the transforming power of God. Don't hide it from others who desperately need the hope you have to offer. Let your light shine through your words and deeds.

We're supposed to hide God's Word—
not our testimony—in our hearts.

The best bridge between
hope and despair is often
a good night's sleep.

*It is vain for you to rise up
early, to sit up late, to eat
the bread of sorrows: for so
he giveth his beloved sleep.*

PSALM 127:2 KJV

Back to the Basics

It's hard to remember the basics. We know we should take care of ourselves, but with so much to do in any given day we tend to place ourselves last on our list. Our need for sleep ends up at the very bottom of that list.

That brings trouble. Our problems are magnified when we're worn out. During a rough night, molehills have a way of looking like mountains. We need our allotted measure of rest in order to see things clearly.

If you've been having trouble sleeping, try these suggestions: Get some exercise during the day, but not just before you go to bed. Avoid all caffeinated products after 3 PM, or so. Try to keep to a regular sleep/wake schedule. Experts believe this is often overlooked. Avoid the news. Try reading a relaxing book or magazine. Finally, read some scripture—and talk to God.

*Take care of yourself by resting
your body, soul, and spirit.*

Some people succeed
because they are destined
to, but most people
succeed because they
are determined to.

*Having done all, to stand.
Stand therefore.*

EPHESIANS 6:13-14 KJV

Standing Firm

If you ever determined to see a project, business venture, or ministry goal come to pass, you probably began with such an enormous amount of passion and energy that you surprised yourself. Nothing stood in your way. You were even eager to put in long days and nights to make a go of it. Then, suddenly, everything came to a halt. Maybe the materials went out of stock, bureaucratic red tape snarled, or suddenly the funds evaporated. What did you do?

Those who believe in the wisdom of the Bible know this would be a good time to stand, resolute and firm, on the God's promises. Philippians 4:13 tells us that we can do all things through Christ, Psalm 23 assures us that God will supply all our needs, and 2 Timothy 1:7 reminds us that fear does not come from God.

With God as your strength, you can stand firm in the face of adversity.

The happiest people
are those who do
the most for others.

*Carry each other's burdens,
and in this way you will
fulfill the law of Christ.*

GALATIANS 6:2

The Happiest People

Booker T. Washington knew what he was talking about. For eighteen years—without a break of any kind—he worked to establish the Tuskegee Institute, one of the few schools for African Americans in the country at that time. When, at the insistence of several people, Washington reluctantly took a vacation, he slept for fifteen hours a day!

That's doing for others. When we help others, we reap a twofold benefit: We fulfill the law of Christ, and we find joy and satisfaction that few other experiences offer. Have you met a genuine servant of God who was bored? No way! They have learned the secret of living for others, never at a loss for something rewarding to do.

Many carry burdens that sap energy and kill the spirit. When we grab hold of the vision of lifting burdens, we can change lives, even ours!

Find a way to serve others—
and bring joy to your own life.

No passion so effectually
robs the mind of all
its powers of acting
and reasoning as fear.

You will keep in perfect peace
him whose mind is steadfast,
because he trusts in you.

ISAIAH 26:3

No Fear

You're walking down a dark city street late at night, cautiously aware of everything around you, trying not to look vulnerable and afraid. One more block, then the hotel and safety. Then you hear the sound of footsteps from behind. Adrenaline floods your body. Your mind freezes. Gone is every bit of advice you ever heard about protecting yourself in such a situation. That's fear.

Fear cripples us. Sudden fear stops us dead in our tracks, and ongoing, nagging fear keeps us from moving forward. Certain fears become a self-fulfilling prophecy—we fear failure in sports, at work, or in our relationships, and sure enough, we fail. When will we learn?

Keep your life in perfect peace. Set your mind unwavering in your trust in God. When you feel fear overcoming you, give it to God before it has a chance to settle in and disturb your peace.

You have a choice: peace or fear.
Which will it be?

Who finds a faithful
friend finds a treasure.

*If one falls down, his friend
can help him up. But pity
the man who falls and has
no one to help him up!*

ECCLESIASTES 4:10

True Friendship

A true friend is one who knows all your faults and loves you anyway. We all long for a friend like that, a person with whom we can share our secret dreams, fears, and insecurities—a person who will never abandon us even if we mess up, lose everything, or become a permanent burden.

Of course, if that's what we're looking for, then we have the whole process backwards. Far more important than *finding* a true friend is *being* a true friend. We need to be the kind of friend who never gives up, even when we've been hurt, misunderstood, or rejected. We also need to be the kind of friend who lovingly confronts and corrects.

Take a good look at the kind of friend you are, and develop openness in your relationships that removes all fear of abandonment or discovery. Be the one who accepts and loves unconditionally.

Friendship is often the glue that keeps us from falling apart.

I've suffered a great
many catastrophes in
my life. Most of them
never happened.

*I will lie down and sleep in
peace, for you alone, O LORD,
make me dwell in safety.*

PSALM 4:8

Save Your Suffering

So many of us have suffered needlessly from catastrophes that never actually happened. Our daughter starts dating an older boy against our will; we just *know* she'll end up pregnant and alone. Our son finally gets his driver's license; we're *sure* his friends will lead him into reckless driving. An enormous corporation gobbles up the little company we work for; we're *certain* that we'll be the one they decide to lay off. We suffer for months, allowing imagined scenarios like these to shatter our peace and our dreams for the future.

What kind of existence is that? Certainly not the kind we were intended to live. When we start playing at make-believe as adults, the game becomes a serious one that can interfere with our mental, spiritual, and physical well-being. Shut down your overactive mind, let go of imaginary tragedies, and learn to lie down and sleep in peace.

Save the suffering for the big—and real—stuff.

If peace be in the heart,
the wildest winter storm
is full of solemn beauty.

*The peace of God, which
transcends all understanding,
will guard your hearts and your
minds in Christ Jesus.*

PHILIPPIANS 4:7

Chasing the Storms

What makes storm-chasers tick—you know, those crazy people who race after ominous clouds, hoping and praying that a tornado will form? Meanwhile, sane people are scrambling for cover in storm cellars, ditches, or any other strong, sturdy shelter they can find. In reality, storm-chasers are not crazy, though they seem that way. Many are mentally sound meteorologists and scientists who simply look at storms from a different perspective than the rest of us. They understand the risks they take, but their goals make those risks worthwhile.

There are spiritual storm-chasers in the world too. They aren't afraid to take risks for the kingdom of God. Their perspective differs from ours; their experiences and Bible reading have revealed a God of safety. They know the storms will not overtake them unless the Lord allows it. The higher purposes of God make every risk they take worthwhile.

The peace of God enables us to ride out the most severe storms.

If you keep watch over your hearts, and listen for the voice of God and learn of Him, in one short hour you can learn more from Him than you could learn from man in a thousand years.

Whether you turn to the right or to the left, your ears will hear a voice behind you, saying, "This is the way; walk in it."

That Still Small Voice

When we first come into a life of faith, we often let our passion for the things of God overtake His direction. We want so much to *do* things for Him that we fail to hear that still, small voice telling us *what* He wants done. Usually after we've made more than our share of mistakes—we settle down and learn to hear Him. Fortunately, He's merciful and keeps us from making complete fools of ourselves.

Do we hear Him audibly? Rarely. Most often, God reveals His direction through an inner knowing that lines up with biblical principles and an understanding of His nature. We place that in the context of what He's doing *now* nearby, and we follow Him. Are the youth in your church on fire for God? That may be where He's calling you to work. Find Him at work, and follow His direction.

Learning to hear God's voice should be one of our primary goals.

Debt is the worst poverty.

*The borrower is servant
to the lender.*

PROVERBS 22:7

No More Debt

If you're in debt, get out of it now, before you become so accustomed to it that it seems normal. Others may say, "Well, that's just the way it is," they'll say. "It's impossible to make ends meet without going into debt."

Don't believe it. If you've come to rely on credit cards, or you can't image a time when you won't have at least one car to pay off, then it will be hard to change your way of thinking, no doubt about it. Paying down debt *can* be done. Start by acknowledging the problem—to yourself, your spouse, and to God—and then seek out a *Christian* debt counseling service. Other services do a fine job, as far as they go, but Christian counselors go back to the God's Word. With that foundation, the lessons you learn last a lifetime, long after you've erased that last debt.

Freedom from debt returns the control of your finances to you.

The best thing about
the future is that it comes
only one day at a time.

We are being renewed day by day.

2 CORINTHIANS 4:16

God of the Second Chance

We hear of the God of the second chance—the One who gives us an opportunity to get it right after we've blown it. In reality, He's the God of the *daily* chance. Fresh and new, every day offers the opportunity to forget the past, to decide to live right, and start all over. That's an enormously significant gift.

Each day also offers us an opportunity to improve ourselves and deepen our relationships with God and others. Maturity and deeper spirituality result from a consistent, and daily renewing of our minds and lives. Sometimes we become discouraged, thinking we should be more mature or more spiritual, but growth does not occur overnight.

Start renewing yourself today—begin a daily Bible reading plan, get up earlier to spend time in prayer, read in an inspirational book, or volunteer your time and gifts to a ministry.

*Think of each day as a special gift
from God: the gift of renewal.*

Never fear the shadows.
They simply mean
there's a light shining
somewhere nearby.

*O Lord, you are my light!
You make my darkness bright.*

2 SAMUEL 22:29 TLB

Light In the Shadows

None of us is immune to experiencing periods of darkness, sometimes prolonged periods. Once we have responded to the God's light, however, we need never again fear the darkness because His light is never extinguished. What's more, other believers carry His light with them and offer hope to us during those times in the shadows.

We all have the responsibility–and the matchless opportunity–to reflect His light into the dark places of other people, and thus help them to see their situation. We also have the task of shining light into places darkened by sin, places to which people have retreated in an effort to deny or hide the wrong in their lives. The darkness they once sought as a cover blinds them. By blowing their cover and shedding light on their transgression, you are offering them the only hope they have for genuine emotional and spiritual freedom.

Search for the source of light
that is making the shadows.

Give your problems
to God; He will be
up all night anyway.

Even the very hairs of
your head are all numbered.
So don't be afraid; you are worth
more than many sparrows.

MATTHEW 10:30-31

Worthy in God's Eyes

One problem that robs us of our peace is our ongoing struggle with self-worth. We easily forget that our worth does not come from outside ourselves. We're barraged with messages that compel us to find our identity in our career, our salary, or our appearance. Even in our own circle of friends, our self-worth depends on how our kids turn out, whether we'll be vacationing in Europe this year, or how many trophies and awards our family has accumulated.

The enemy of our soul would have us devalue ourselves, or value ourselves for the wrong reasons. The real truth comes from the One who loves us and values us simply because we are. Even our gifts and talents have nothing to do with our worth, and everything to do with His goodness, kindness, and generosity in giving them. Our personal worth comes from God alone.

We make peace with ourselves when we recognize who we are in God.

This world belongs to the man who is wise enough to change his mind in the presence of facts.

Whoever heeds correction gains understanding.

PROVERBS 15:32

Accepting Correction

Learning to accept correction moves us toward maturity. Children and teenagers exhibit their immaturity by balking whenever anyone—especially a parent, but often teachers and others in authority as well—attempts to correct them. If the ability to accept correction is not nurtured and developed, the result is an adult who either will be hampered in their efforts to succeed or will become embittered toward their supervisors and coworkers.

Sometimes correction is given in the wrong spirit. Even so, we are not responsible for another person's attitude, only for accepting or rejecting what he has to say. That your boss points out an error in a demeaning way does not invalidate your mistake. A mature person will accept the correction, ignore the put-down, and make whatever changes the correction requires. In doing so, they gain not only knowledge, but also a deeper level of understanding and wisdom.

The ability to admit you're wrong keeps you humble—and growing.

Call on God, but row
away from the rocks.

Wisdom and good judgment
live together, for wisdom knows
where to discover knowledge
and understanding.

PROVERBS 8:12 TLB

Growing Wise

You've no doubt heard, "She doesn't have the sense she was born with." Maybe you've even said it—or heard it said about you. We're all born with a measure of good sense, but our judgment needs to be cultivated as we grow. We don't just wake up one day and decide we're going to have better judgment; and we can't take a correspondence course or enroll in a seminar on developing good sense. We acquire good sense when we consciously begin to search for knowledge and understanding.

How do we do that? By regular, thoughtful reading of the Bible and applying the principles we discover there, to begin with. When we saturate our minds with Scripture—and our spirits with the things of God—wisdom grows. Then, in crisis, we can draw on that well of wisdom.

Make sure you that as you journey through life, you add to your well of good sense!

The stars are constantly
shining, but often we
do not see them until
the dark hours.

God is our refuge and strength,
an ever-present help in trouble.

PSALM 46:1

God, Our Refuge

Do you know what it means to have God as your refuge? Imagine an old European castle, the kind impenetrable to marauding warriors. Now imagine that castle surrounded by a tightly packed company of powerful, angelic beings, weapons drawn, ready to defend. You, of course, are safe and sound in the innermost chamber of this fortress.

That's what it's like to have God as our refuge. A storm with the force of Hurricane Andrew could barrel through. Attila the Hun and his band of invaders could come at us with murderous intent, and we'd be sheltered and protected. Our God is a safe haven from all the troubles of life.

The next time the winds howl, the lightning flashes, and the thunder roars above—when the enemy attacks— remember that you are safe within, that a host of angelic warriors surrounds you.

You can be an example to others by your calm demeanor in the face of trouble.

Some gentleman says I have been a tailor. That does not disconcert me in the least; for when I was a tailor I had the reputation of being a good one, and making close fits; I was always punctual with my customers, and always did good work.

Do you see a man skilled in his work? He will serve before kings; he will not serve before obscure men.

PROVERBS 22:29

Serve Before Kings

A woman who worked as a nanny in the United States was once told by a believing friend that she would one day serve before kings. She chuckled at the thought but never forgot her friend's words. Nearly a decade later, this nanny had become so highly regarded in her work that an employment agency called and asked her if she would be available to serve as a nanny for the children of a European prince. She jumped at the chance—and had many opportunities to share the gospel with royalty.

You never know when the very skills you possess may be used for a higher purpose than you could ever imagine. Don't take lightly the gifts and talents you've been given; build on them until you do even the common things uncommonly well. As you serve the King of Kings, you may serve earthly kings as well.

The most common skills become priceless when used for the kingdom.

You can accomplish
more in one hour with
God than in one lifetime
without Him.

*Walk in wisdom . . .
redeeming the time.*

COLOSSIANS 4:5 NKJV

Too Busy Not to Pray

Martin Luther spent a good deal of time in prayer each day, except when he had an exceptionally busy schedule. Then, he would pray twice as long. That sounds backwards, and so foreign to the way most of us live. On our really busy days, we rush through our devotional time . . . or skip it. We're not likely to go down in history as great spiritual leaders or reformers of the church, either.

Spending more time with God doesn't make Him more willing to grant our wishes, nor does it make Him like us more. Instead, the time we spend in prayer changes us, allows us access to wisdom from above, and helps steer us in the right direction. Luther made his plans subject to God's will, knowing that his own participation in those plans would be effective only to the extent that he relied on God.

An unusually busy day? Try getting up earlier and praying longer.

Enthusiasm is contagious.
It's difficult to remain neutral
or indifferent in the presence
of a positive thinker.

*Finally, brethren, whatever is
true . . . honorable . . . right . . .
pure . . . lovely . . . of good
repute, if there is any excellence
and if anything worthy of praise,
dwell on these things.*

PHILIPPIANS 4:8 NASB

In with the Positive!

Medical, mental health, and spiritual authorities all agree that our thought life, in large measure, determines the quality of our lives. For example, the more we think successful thoughts, the more likely we are to be successful. Constantly thinking that we will fail, however, will almost certainly produce failure.

Why? For one thing, as we promote positive thoughts, the underlying truth of those thoughts settles into the subconscious portion of our mind, creating a deep well of "honorable . . . right . . . pure . . . lovely" beliefs that we can draw on throughout our lives. In addition, right thinking crowds out wrong thinking. Our minds can only handle so much at one time, and positive thoughts leave no room for negative thoughts. The emotional, physical, and spiritual benefits are substantial as the truth of who we are in God emerges, transforming our life.

Be prepared to receive fresh insights as you consciously change your thought life.

The art of being wise
is the art of knowing
what to overlook.

A man's wisdom gives him
patience; it is to his glory
to overlook an offense.

PROVERBS 19:11

Off the Hook

When another person offends you, it's human nature to want some retaliation. One of our goals in life, however, is to gradually replace our base human nature with a higher spiritual nature, one that resembles the divine. That means we need to train ourselves to overlook the offenses of others, remembering that our attempts to draw a person into a life of faith require us to turn the other cheek.

As usual, the best way to understand the significance of this is for you to turn the tables on yourself. Can you recall a time when you offended another person—and they shrugged it off, valuing your friendship more than their hurt? Or maybe they didn't, and an unforgiving friend walked away forever, leaving you feeling even worse about your offense.

Be quick to let others off the hook. You never know when you'll find yourself *on* the hook, and in need of forgiveness.

Learn to become a thick-skinned friend.

He only is exempt
from failures who
makes no efforts.

Be strong, courageous, and firm,
fear not . . . for it is the Lord
your God Who goes with you;
He will not fail you or forsake you.

DEUTERONOMY 31:6 AMP

Don't Give Up!

How do you know you've failed at a project? Is it when the ink is dry, the presentation has been made, or your friend has rejected your witness for the umpteenth time? What may look like failure could actually be an extended pause that allows you to see how strong, courageous, and firm you really are. Consider this a first failure, not a final one. The ultimate failure comes only if you give up for good.

Think long and hard before you do that. Many a blockbuster bestseller has been rejected dozens of times before finally seeing print—and many a friend has come to God after the umpteenth-plus time they were invited. The sports world abounds with athletes who refused to pack it in, even after suffering humiliating defeats before tens of thousands of spectators. All these stories tell us not to give up too soon.

Where failure is tolerated, success finds its greatest opportunity.

Nothing great was ever done without much enduring.

Do not, therefore, fling away your fearless confidence, for it carries a great and glorious compensation of reward. For you have need of steadfast patience and endurance, so that you may perform and fully accomplish the will of God.

HEBREWS 10:35-36 AMP

The Fruit of Endurance

There's no better example of endurance throughout history—especially endurance leading to a glorious result—than the crucifixion of Jesus. We meditate on the agony He experienced both in His body and in His spiritual separation from the Father, in tears at the thought of anyone enduring all that for our sake. Then we remember the glorious result, freedom from the grip of sin and death.

Sometimes, the things we have to suffer feel more like boot camp than ministry. People bark and curse at us, and then expect us to jump through hoops for them. At the end of the day, we're covered from head to toe with the muck of the world. This is the abundant life? Well, yes—it's a phase of the abundant life that trains us to endure to the end. When boot camp ends, you'll be equipped to meet the enemy head on.

*Our endurance will often accomplish
more than we can ever imagine.*

Acknowledgements

(6) Francois de la Rochefoucauld, (8,24,30) Will Rogers, (10) Immanuel Kant, (12,16,18,20,22,62,76,90,102,104,124,138,144) Anonymous, (14) Dwight Lyman Moody, (26) Owen Felltham, (28) Latin Proverb, (32,46,126) Mark Twain, (34) Albert Einstein, (36) George Bernard Shaw, (38,120) Booker T. Washington, (40) Publilius Syrus, (42) James Albery, (44) Henry Ford , (48) Robert Browning, (50) Winston Churchill, (52) John Flavel, (54) Joseph Joubert, (56) Victor Hugo, (58,96) Charles Spurgeon, (60) Joseph Addison, (64) Mother Teresa, (66) John F. Kennedy, (68) Theodore Roosevelt, (70) Ronald Reagan, (72) Jeremy Taylor, (74,94,132) Sir Thomas Fuller, (78) Blaise Pascal, (80) Jean Nicolas Grou, (82) Mary Webb, (84) Thomas Sprat, (86) Cicero, (88) Nathaniel Hawthorne, (92,134) Abraham Lincoln, (98) Maria Thusick, (100) Johann Wolfgang von Goethe, (106) Helen Keller, (108) Martin Luther, (110) John Bunyan, (112) Franklin D. Roosevelt, (114) William Shedd, (116) Heraclitus, (118) Heraclitus, (122) Edmund Burke, (128) C.F. Richardson, (130) Johann Tauler, (136) Ruth E. Renkel, (140) Thomas Carlyle, (142) Indian Proverb, (146) President Andrew Johnson, (148,158) Ralph Waldo Emerson, (150) Friedrich Wilhelm Nietzsche, (152) William James, (154) Richard Whatley, (156) Catherine of Siena.

References

Unless otherwise indicated, all Scripture quotations are taken from the *Holy Bible, New International Version*® NIV®. Copyright © 1973, 1978, 1984 by International Bible Society. Used by permission of Zondervan Publishing House. All rights reserved.

Scripture quotations marked AMP are taken from *The Amplified Bible. Old Testament* copyright © 1965, 1987 by Zondervan Corporation, Grand Rapids Michigan. *New Testament* copyright © 1958, 1987 by The Lockman Foundation, La Habra, California. Used by permission.

Scripture quotations marked KJV are taken from the *King James Version* of the Bible.

Scripture quotations marked NASB are taken from the *New American Standard Bible.* Copyright © The Lockman Foundation 1960, 1962, 1963, 1968, 1971, 1972, 1973, 1975, 1977, 1995. Used by permission.

Scripture quotations marked NKJV are taken from *The New King James Version.* Copyright © 1979, 1980, 1982, Thomas Nelson, Inc.

Verses marked TLB are taken from *The Living Bible* © 1971. Used by permission of Tyndale House Publishers, Inc., Wheaton, Illinois 60189. All rights reserved.

Scripture quotations marked THE MESSAGE are taken from *The Message,* copyright © by Eugene H. Peterson, 1993, 1994, 1995, 1996. Used by permission of NavPress Publishing Group.

Additional copies of this book and other
titles from Honor Books
are available from your local bookstore.

Also Available:

The Pocket Devotional for Mothers
The Pocket Devotional for Teens
The Pocket Devotional for Women

Other Honor Books titles you might enjoy:

Everyday Prayers for Everyday Cares
God's Little Book of Promises
God's Little Devotional Book
God's Little Devotional Book–Special Gift Edition
God's Little Devotional Journal
God's Little Instruction Book
God's Little Lessons on Life
Quiet Moments with God

If you have enjoyed this book, or if it has impacted your life,
we would like to hear from you.

Please contact us at:

Honor Books
Department E
P.O. Box 55388
Tulsa, Oklahoma 74155
Or by e-mail at *info@honorbooks.com*